BONE BROTH BREAKTHROUGH

Dr. Josh Axe

NOTICE TO READER

This book is not intended to provide medical advice or to take the place of medical advice and treatment from your personal physician. Readers are advised to consult their doctors or qualified health professionals regarding specific health questions. Neither the publisher nor the author takes responsibility for possible health consequences of any person reading or following the information in this book. All readers, especially those taking prescription or over-the-counter medications, should consult their physicians before beginning any nutrition or supplement program.

† These statements have not been evaluated by the Food and Drug Administration. This product is not intended to diagnose, treat, cure or prevent any disease.

CONTENTS

ABOUT

DR. JOSH AXE

Dr. Josh Axe, DNM, DC, CNS, is a doctor of natural medicine, doctor of chiropractic and clinical nutritionist with a passion to help people get well using food as medicine and operates one of the worlds largest natural health websites: www.DrAxe.com.

He is the author of the groundbreaking health book *Eat Dirt*, which uncovers the hidden causes and cures of leaky gut syndrome. Dr. Axe is an expert in digestive health, functional medicine, natural remedies and dietary strategies for healing. He has been featured on many television shows, including the Dr. Oz Show, CBS and NBC, and has his own *Eat Dirt* program running on select PBS TV stations.

Dr. Axe founded one of the largest functional medicine clinics in the world, in Nashville, TN, and has been a physician for many professional athletes.

DrAxe.com is one of the most visited websites worldwide for healthy recipes, herbal remedies, nutrition and fitness advice, essential oils, and natural supplements.

CHAPTER 1

BONE BROTH IS NOT HYPE:
IT'S A BIG HELP

Considered to be one of the most ancient and remarkable nutritional substances on the planet, bone broth is a beneficial "elixir" made from simmered animal bones. Not only does bone broth taste great and provide numerous nutrients and beneficial compounds, but it's versatile and easy to use in many recipes.

Yet the vast majority of the general public passes up the opportunity to boost its health with bone broth, often unaware of how incredibly good it is for you. Instead, if any broth is consumed, it's often the store-bought, processed, sodium-filled, nutritionally bankrupt versions.

Bone broth is a great place to find valuable amino acids, collagen, gelatin and trace minerals. In fact, there are dozens of different nutrients found within bone broth, many of which can't be obtained easily from other commonly eaten foods.

Here are six of the key nutritional compounds found in bone broth

BOOST YOUR BODY WITH BONE BROTH'S NUTRITION

Bone broth could be called "nature's multivitamin." How so exactly? It's packed with:

- Over 19 easy-to-absorb, essential and non-essential amino acids (the building blocks of proteins)
- Collagen/gelatin, which helps form connective tissue
- Nutrients that support digestive functions, immunity and brain health

Did you get that? It literally boosts every part of your body, from your gut to your brain, from your muscles to your ligaments.

It's also relatively low in calories, yet very high in minerals and other chemical compounds that many people lack. There's no doubt that bone broth makes a great everyday addition to your diet.

1. GLYCOSAMINOGLYCANS

Glycosaminoglycans (GAG) have the primary role of maintaining and supporting collagen and elastin that take up the spaces between bones and various fibers. GAGs are supportive for digestive health since they help restore the intestinal lining, which is why a deficiency in these nutrients has been linked to digestive challenges. † (1)

Several important GAGs are found in bone broth, including glucosamine, hyaluronic acid and chondroitin sulfate.

2. GLUCOSAMINE

There are two main types of naturally occurring glucosamine: hydrochloride and sulfate. Both help keep up the integrity of cartilage, which is the rubbery substance within joints that acts like a natural cushion. Studies show that glucosamine can become depleted as we get older, so supplements are often used to support joint health. †

An easy and relatively inexpensive way to obtain glucosamine naturally is from drinking more bone broth, which helps support cartilage health, acting as an alternative to pricey glucosamine supplements. (2) Consuming more glucosamine can help support joint health, flexibility and comfort. †

1. www.naturalmedicinejournal.com/journal/2015-04/n-acetylglucosamine-treatment-inflammatory-bowel-disease
2. www.webmd.com/vitamins-and-supplements/lifestyle-guide-11/supplement-guide-glucosamine

3. HYALURONIC ACID

Found throughout connective, epithelial (skin) and neural tissues, hyaluronic acid contributes to cell proliferation, differentiation and mitigation, allowing our cells to perform various functions throughout the body as needed. It offers support for multiple skin types and promotes healthy aging, cell rejuvenation and skin firmness. † (3)

4. CHONDROITIN SULFATE

Chondroitin sulfate is a beneficial glycosaminoglycan found in the cartilage within the joints of all animals. It's often used to support joint health and comfort, especially in combination with glucosamine.

Studies have found that supplementing with chondroitin supports healthy inflammation response as well as cardiovascular health, bone health, skin health and healthy cholesterol levels. † (4)

5. MINERALS AND ELECTROLYTES

Bone broth provides essential minerals, including electrolytes, all provided in an easy-to-absorb form. Electrolytes found within bone broth include calcium, magnesium and potassium (not to mention many other minerals, such as phosphorus), which are important for supporting healthy circulation, bone density,

3. www.ncbi.nlm.nih.gov/pmc/articles/PMC3583886/
4. www.webmd.com/vitamins-supplements/ingredientmono-744-chondroitin%20sulfate.aspx?activeingredientid=744&activeingredient-name=chondroitin%20sulfate

nerve-signaling functions, heart health and digestive health. When added sodium levels are kept low, bone broth contains an ideal balance of sodium and potassium to support cellular health and efficiency. †

6. COLLAGEN

Collagen is the main structural protein found within the human body that helps form connective tissue and "seals" the protective lining of the gastrointestinal tract. It's also the gel-like, smooth structure that covers and holds our bones together, allowing us to glide and move freely.

Irritation within the gut impairs normal digestive functions and causes permeability, allowing particles to pass into the bloodstream, known as leaky gut. †

As a rich source of gelatin, bone broth protects and seals the mucosal lining of the GI tract, which means it improves nutrient absorption and also helps keep particles from leaching out where they shouldn't be.

As a complex protein, collagen contains a whopping 19 amino acids, with a mix of both non-essential (also called conditional) and essential types. Many of the amino acids found within collagen must be obtained from our diets since our bodies cannot make them on their own. †

KEY AMINO ACIDS FOUND WITHIN COLLAGEN INCLUDE:

PROLINE

- Proline, which is the chief component of collagen, is essential for building integrity for healthy skin, hair and nails. †
- Proline is essential for building the gut lining and facilitating digestive function, yet most people are lacking this amino acid in their diets because they don't consume organ meats or bone broth on a regular basis. †
- Proline is needed for tissue repair within the joints and arteries, plus it helps support healthy blood pressure levels. †
- As a key component of collagen found within joints, proline buffers our bodies from the effects of vibration or shock and helps us hold on to valuable cartilage as we get older. † (5)
- Proline supports healthy cardiovascular function. †

GLUTAMINE

- Glutamine supports the body in the maintenance of healthy muscle tissue during and after periods of exercise, and helps with muscular fatigue. †
- Research shows that glutamine supports digestive health, healthy immune system response and energy levels. † (6)
- It also provides "fuel" to our cells and supports a healthy intestinal lining. †
- It supports synthesis of glutathione, one of the body's most powerful antioxidants. †

5. www.biology.arizona.edu/biochemistry/problem_sets/aa/proline.html
6. www.aminoacid-studies.com/amino-acids/glutamine-and-glutamic-acid.html

GLYCINE

- Approximately one-third of the protein found in collagen is glycine. †
- One of glycine's most important roles is helping to form muscle tissue by converting glucose into usable energy that feeds muscle cells. †
- This amino acid is found in high quantities in muscles, the skin and various tissues. †
- Research shows glycine has important roles in digestion and central nervous system function. † (7)
- Glycine promotes detoxification and cleansing. †

ARGININE

- Arginine breaks down into nitric oxide within the body, which is an important compound for arterial and cardiovascular health. † (8)
- Nitric oxide allows for better vasodilation, meaning the widening of arteries and relaxation of muscle cells and blood vessels that allows for better circulation. †
- Arginine also helps the body make more protein from other amino acids, which is important for repairing muscle tissue, normal wound healing, sparing tissue wasting, boosting the metabolism, and aiding in proper growth and development. †

7. www.webmd.com/vitamins-supplements/ingredientmono-1072-glycine.aspx?activeingredientid=1072&activeingredientname=glycine
8. www.aminoacid-studies.com/amino-acids/arginine.html

CHAPTER 2

BONE BROTH & COLLAGEN BY THE NUMBERS

Bone broth is very versatile and can be made using bones from just about any type of animal. The bones are usually simmered for about 24–48 hours, often mixed with other nutrient-dense foods, such as vegetables, herbs and spices, and uses an acidic liquid like apple cider vinegar to liberate key minerals.

Many people prefer one type of bone broth over another.

But you can simply use bones from any animal you have left over after cooking and then remove the meat, or buy bones from a farmer's market, local health food store, a butcher or online.

Some of the most popular types of bones to use come from cows, veal, lamb, bison, venison, chicken, duck, goose, turkey or fish.

BEEF BONE BROTH

- Beef broth is one of the richest, most savory and nutrient-packed bone broths and is high in type 1 and type 3 collagen.
- Often made using veggies, herbs and spices, including garlic, celery, carrots, onions and even apple cider.
- High in bone marrow and amino acids, especially when you include some larger bones that contain a high amount of cartilage and collagen.

CHICKEN AND TURKEY BONE BROTH

- You've likely had chicken soup or broth many times in your life, but the homemade stuff is far superior to any canned variety.
- Many homemade chicken broths are made using chicken feet, knuckles, skin, giblets or other organ parts, which are high in healthy fatty acids and collagen type 2.

FISH BONE BROTH

- Fish bone broth has been used in Asia for thousands of years.
- The broth made from fish tends to be milder and lighter, since the bones are smaller.
- Fish stock is a great addition to soups, stews and noodle dishes.
- It's a great source of iodine, calcium, amino acids and healthy fats (especially when you use wild-caught fish).
- It's a good alternative to chicken or beef stocks if you don't eat meat or have easier access to whole fish.

Meanwhile, there are at least 16 **types of collagen** within the human body, but 80 percent to 90 percent of the collagen consists of types 1, 2 and 3. (9)

9. www.ncbi.nlm.nih.gov/books/NBK21582/

Type 1:

- The most abundant and strongest type of collagen within the human body is type 1
- Made of eosinophilic fibers and found in tendons, ligaments, bone, the dermis (skin) and various organs
- Type 1 collagen is used to form bones and support wound healing since it's extra strong and capable of being stretched without tearing †

Type 2:

- Cartilage within our joints is mainly composed of type 2 collagen, the primary protein found in our connective tissues
- Researchers at Harvard's Beth Israel Deaconess Medical Center in Boston found that supplementing with type 2 collagen supports healthy inflammation response † (10)
- Other studies have found that people who supplement their diets with type 2 collagen show significant enhancements in daily activities and a general improvement in their quality of life † (11)
- Type 2 collagen is primarily found in chicken and turkey broth and is also the best for repairing and sealing the gut lining †
- If you want to support digestive and immune system health, make sure you get type 2 collagen in your daily diet †

Type 3:

- Type 3 collagen is a major component of the extracellular matrix that makes up our organs and skin
- It helps give skin its elasticity and firmness, plus forms our blood vessels and tissue within the heart †

10. www.ncbi.nlm.nih.gov/pubmed/8378772
11. www.ncbi.nlm.nih.gov/pubmed/19847319

CHAPTER 3

SIX REASONS TO CONSUME BONE BROTH EVERY DAY

In one way or another, just about every culture throughout history has used a form of bone broth to improve health and support a healthy immune system. In ancient China, for example, gelatin was prized as a natural way to maintain muscle strength, bone density and ease of movement into older age, since it protects joints, bones and muscle tissue from damage. † (1)

Our ancestors valued bone broth as a "nose-to-tail" approach to using all parts of an animal, including the bone marrow and skin that are often discarded today. Using these parts was an inexpensive, convenient way to obtain an abundance of minerals, proteins and other nutrients while also flavoring recipes and avoiding waste.

According to a report in the *New York Times*, many years ago people made bone broth by dropping fire-heated rocks into the stomachs of whatever animals they managed to kill. Years later, with the invention of stoves and pots, bone broth became easier than ever to make and turned into a "staple in virtually every corner of the culinary world." (2)

Although animal ligaments, joints and bones might not seem very appealing to eat, they are highly nutritious parts of the animal that hold ingredients not readily available in muscle meat or plant foods. Throughout history, bone broth was sipped on not only because it was comforting, but also because it was said to help calm the nerves, improve energy and promote healthy aging. †

Up until recently, western culture has mostly ignored the benefits of traditional bone broths. Many people are hesitant to consume

1. https://www.jadeinstitute.com/jade/bone-broth-health-building.php
2. www.nytimes.com/2015/01/07/dining/bone-broth-evolves-from-prehistoric-food-to-paleo-drink.html?_r=0

animal parts other than meat or to cook with bones, marrow and cartilage. Luckily, today more emphasis is being placed on the importance of obtaining nutrients naturally, rather than turning to synthetic supplements. Bone broth is making a huge comeback and even being called a "superfood."

Over the past century, more and more research has shown us that overall health highly depends on the state of the microbiome, or the mix of microorganisms living within the intestinal tract. Most systems, if not every system, of the body are interrelated to the health of our guts, which are dependent on the state of our microbiomes. That's because an unbalanced ratio of bad-to-good bacteria, fungus, yeast and microbes living within the gut alters how the immune system works. †

In fact, a very large percentage of our immune system activity — about 70 percent to 80 percent — actually resides in the digestive tract, which holds trillions of bacteria and other microbes that affect nearly every bodily function in one way or another.

Because it's chock-full of nutrients and easy to digest (even for people with compromised gut health), bone broth plays a major role in many programs designed to help support digestive functions and nutrient absorption, as well as to restore integrity of the gut lining. This includes the GAPS Diet, the Maker's Diet, the Bone Broth Diet, and other cleansing, fasting or immune support programs. †

† These statements have not been evaluated by the Food and Drug Administration. This product is not intended to diagnose, treat, cure or prevent any disease.

By regularly drinking bone broth or using it in recipes, you can help promote healthy gut integrity while reducing permeability and inflammation. Here are the six major benefits of bone broth. †

1. PROTECTS JOINTS

Bone broth is one of world's best sources of natural collagen, the protein found in animals — in their bones, skin, cartilage, ligaments, tendons and bone marrow. As we get older, our joints naturally experience wear-and-tear, and we become less flexible.

Why does that matter? As we age, cartilage diminishes as it gets attacked by antibodies (age-related degradation of joint cartilage). As bone broth simmers, collagen from the animal parts leaches into the broth and becomes readily absorbable to help restore cartilage.

One of the most valuable components of bone broth is gelatin, which acts like a soft cushion between bones that helps them "glide" without friction. Gelatin also provides us with building blocks that are needed to form and maintain strong bones, helping take pressure off of aging joints and supporting healthy bone mineral density. †

Research done by the Department of Nutrition and Sports Nutrition for Athletes at Penn State University found that when athletes supplemented with collagen over the course of 24 weeks, the majority showed significant improvements in joint comfort and a decrease in factors that negatively impacted athletic performance. † (3)

3. www.ncbi.nlm.nih.gov/pubmed/18416885

2. GOOD FOR THE GUT †

Studies show that gelatin is beneficial for restoring strength of the gut lining and fighting food sensitivities (such as to wheat or dairy), helping with the growth of probiotics ("good bacteria) in the gut, and supporting healthy inflammation levels in the digestive tract. A report published in the *Journal of Clinical Gastroenterology* found that gelatin effectively supports intestinal health and integrity. † (4)

Bone broth is easily digested and soothing to the digestive system, unlike many other foods that can be difficult to fully break down. After all, a food is really only useful if we have the means of absorbing its nutrients.

Studies have found that in individuals with digestive imbalances, serum concentrations of collagen are decreased. (5) Because the amino acids in collagen build the tissue that lines the colon and entire GI tract, supplementing with collagen can support healthy digestive function. †

3. MAINTAINS HEALTHY SKIN †

Collagen helps form elastin and other compounds within skin that are responsible for maintaining skin's youthful tone, texture and appearance. Collagen integrity is accredited with helping reduce the visible signs of wrinkles, decreasing puffiness and fighting various other signs of aging. Many people report a decrease in cellulite when consuming foods and supplements containing collagen, since cellulite forms due to a lack of connective tissue, allowing skin to lose its firm tone. †

4. www.ncbi.nlm.nih.gov/pmc/articles/PMC3358810/
5. www.ncbi.nlm.nih.gov/pubmed/14600124
6. www.ncbi.nlm.nih.gov/pubmed/23949208

Double-blind, placebo-controlled studies investigating the age-defending properties of collagen have found that 2.5–5 grams of collagen hydrolysate (CH) used among women aged 35–55 once daily for eight weeks supports skin elasticity, skin moisture, transepidermal water loss (dryness) and skin roughness. At the end of only four weeks, those using collagen showed a statistically significant improvement in comparison to those using a placebo with regard to skin moisture and skin evaporation, plus noticeable decreases in signs of accelerated aging, all with little to no side effects. † (6)

4. SUPPORTS IMMUNE SYSTEM FUNCTION †

One of the most remarkable things about bone broth is its gut supportive benefits, which as described above actually have a holistic effect on the body and support healthy immune system function. †

Leaky gut occurs when undigested particles from foods seep through tiny openings in the weakened intestinal lining and enter the bloodstream, where the immune system detects them and becomes hyperactive. This increases inflammation and leads to dysfunctions all over, as the immune system releases high levels of antibodies that cause an autoimmune-like response and attacks healthy tissue. †

Bone broth is one of the most beneficial foods to consume to restore gut health and therefore support immune system function and healthy inflammation response. Collagen/gelatin and the amino acids proline, glutamine and arginine help seal these openings in the gut lining and support gut integrity.

Traditionally made bone broths are believed to support healthy inflammatory response and normal immune system function. (7, 8) Bone broth can even promote healthy sleep, boost energy during the day and support a healthy mood. †

5. BOOSTS DETOXIFICATION †

Today in the Western world, the average person is exposed to an array of environmental toxins, pesticides, artificial ingredients and chemicals of all sorts. While the human body has its own means of detoxifying itself from heavy metals and other toxic exposures, it often has a hard time keeping up when flooded with an overwhelming amount of chemicals. Bone broth is considered a powerful detoxification agent since it helps the digestive system expel waste and promotes the liver's ability to remove toxins, helps maintain tissue integrity and improves the body's use of antioxidants. †

Bone broth contains potassium and glycine, which support both cellular and liver detoxification. †

Some of the ways in which bone broth boosts detoxification is by supplying sulfur (especially when you add veggies, garlic and herbs to your broth) and glutathione, which is a phase II detoxification agent that lowers oxidative stress. Stanford University's Medicine Preventative Research Center has found that glutathione helps with elimination of fat-soluble compounds, especially heavy metals like mercury and lead. It also helps with the absorption of various nutrients, the use of antioxidants and with liver-cleansing functions. † (9) Bone broth also increases intake of essential minerals, which act like chelators to remove toxins by stopping heavy metals from attaching to mineral receptor sites.

7. www.ncbi.nlm.nih.gov/m/pubmed/11035691/
8. www.ncbi.nlm.nih.gov/pubmed/11035691
9. nutrition.stanford.edu/projects/Glutathione-NACStudy.html

6. AIDS THE METABOLISM AND PROMOTES ANABOLISM †

Bone broth is a great way to obtain more glutathione, which studies show plays important roles in antioxidant defense, nutrient metabolism and regulation of cellular events. A 2004 study published in the *Journal of Nutrition* states that glutathione's roles and benefits include regulating gene expressions, DNA and protein synthesis, cell proliferation and apoptosis, signal transduction, cytokine production, and immune responses. † (10)

Amino acids found in bone broth have numerous metabolic roles, including building and repairing muscle tissue, supporting bone mineral density, boosting nutrient absorption and synthesis, and maintaining muscle and connective tissue health. Glycine found within collagen helps form muscle tissue by converting glucose into usable energy, plus it slows cartilage, tissue and muscle loss associated with aging by improving the body's use of antioxidants. Studies have revealed that glycine protects skeletal muscle loss and stops the expression of genes associated with age-related muscle protein breakdown. † (11)

Glutamine is another amino acid that's important for a healthy metabolism, since it helps us maintain energy by sending nutrients, including nitrogen, to our cells. Arginine also has the role of breaking down nitric oxide that helps improve circulation and sends blood and nutrients to cells throughout the body, improving muscle and tissue integrity and promoting normal wound healing. †

10. www.ncbi.nlm.nih.gov/pubmed/14988435
11. www.ncbi.nlm.nih.gov/pubmed/23835111

CHAPTER 4

HOW TO MAKE A GREAT BONE BROTH

There are a few important basics to consider when making a great bone broth. First, while animal components and water alone can make a simple and healthy broth, combining it all with some select vegetables, herbs and spices appears to have synergistic effects, working together to be more beneficial than either alone.

Speed-wise, it's easy to simply use the animal carcass and bones, but for additional collagen and gelatin benefits, consider using parts including chicken feet and neck. No matter what animal you decide to base your bone broth on, however, from chicken to cow to lamb to fish, make sure that it's as free of chemicals as possible.

The essential ingredients of a solid bone broth, according to bestselling author Sally Fallon, co-founder of the Weston A. Price Foundation, are bones, fat, meat, vegetables and water.

If you're making beef broth or lamb broth, you should brown the meat before putting it into a stock pot. Fish and poultry, meanwhile, are fine to put in a pot without browning first. Then you simply add a bit of apple cider vinegar to your pot to help draw the minerals from the bones.

For added nutrients and flavor, I suggest using sea salt, carrots, onions and celery along with parsley (or even better, Herbs de Provence). To receive additional multisystemic benefits, add ginger, turmeric and other tasty powerful herbs.

As you can see, the options abound for bone broth. You can use different animals as the base, make simple or more complex versions, choose different flavoring ingredients, or even choose the convenient option of a ready-to-mix bone broth protein powder.

IF YOU DO DECIDE TO MAKE BONE BROTH AT HOME, HERE ARE THE STEPS TO TAKE:

1 Choose a large pot for the stovetop or a crockpot. Place the bones into the pot or crockpot and cover with water. (If you're making beef or lamb broth, you should brown the meat before putting it into a stock pot. Fish and poultry, including chicken feet and the neck, are fine to put in a pot without browning first.) Make sure you leave plenty of room for water to boil.

2 Add two tablespoons of apple cider vinegar to water prior to cooking. This helps pull out important nutrients from the bones.

3 Heat slowly, by bringing it to a boil and then reducing the heat to simmer for at least 6 hours. Skim off fat on top as it arises.

4 Now, while 6 hours is the minimum time to extract those valuable nutrients from the bones, chicken bones can cook for 24 hours and beef bones can cook for 48 hours. (Fish stock, using the bones and the head, requires the least amount of time and sometimes one hour is adequate.) Overall, a low temperature and slow cook time are necessary in order to first preserve and then fully extract the nutrients in and around bone.

5 You can also add in vegetables, such as onions, garlic, carrots and celery, for added nutrient value. For standard flavor, add herbs and spices, such as parsley or Herbs de Provence. For an additional kick (and more health benefits), consider adding ginger and turmeric.

6 Remove from heat and allow to cool slightly. Discard solids and strain remainder in a bowl through a colander.

7 Let broth cool to room temperature, cover and chill. Use within a week or freeze for up to 3 months.

CHAPTER 5

BONE BROTH PROTEIN POWDER

What if I told you there was an easy way to receive all of the benefits of bone broth without having to spend hours making it or paying a high price for the frozen variety? That's where Bone Broth Protein Powder comes in. Bone Broth Protein™ † is bone broth liquid that is dehydrated, making it into a concentrated source of high-quality and tasty powder.

This is THE protein powder I recommend to all of my patients because of the incredible health benefits and its convenience and ease of use. As wonderful as bone broth is, preparing and consuming it regularly is a daunting task to say the least. With Bone Broth Protein, one can consume health-giving bone broth in literally seconds with no prep or cleanup at home, work or when traveling.

A quality Bone Broth Protein (not to be confused with bouillon cubes, which are packed with artificial flavorings and sodium) comes with the same benefits of a homemade broth, but it's also just as tolerable for digestion and versatile in so many recipes. In addition, Bone Broth Protein supplies 20 grams of muscle-building protein to support healthy muscle building and maintenance and metabolism. †

THE CONVERSION IS SIMPLE

| 1 SCOOP BONE BROTH PROTEIN | 12 OUNCES OF WATER | 1.5 CUPS BONE BROTH |

† These statements have not been evaluated by the Food and Drug Administration. This product is not intended to diagnose, treat, cure or prevent any disease.

What is the difference between Bone Broth Protein and collagen powder? Most collagen powders on the market today contain types 1 and 3 collagen but don't have the other beneficial nutrients found in chicken bone broth. Bone Broth Protein contains high levels of type 2 collagen but also contains vital minerals, including potassium, magnesium, calcium, selenium, glycosaminoglycans (GAGs), hyaluronic acid, glucosamine and chondroitin.

Because Bone Broth Protein contains higher levels of type 2 collagen (support for the gut, skin, immune system and joints) while bovine collagen contains higher levels of type 1 and 3 collagen (support for hair, skin, bones and muscle), I recommend my patients use both on a daily basis. †

FIVE BIG BENEFITS OF BONE BROTH PROTEIN †

1 **Saves You Time** – Bone Broth Protein is easier than making bone broth yourself at home, not as messy and will give back time to your already busy schedule.

2 **Super Cost-Effective** – If you go out and purchase a container or jar of bone broth liquid from a retailer or your local farmers market, you will pay an average of $5.50 per serving versus paying only $2.25 per serving of Bone Broth Protein. You save twice a much!

3 **Packed with Protein** – With 20 grams of high-quality, easily digestible protein per serving, Bone Broth Protein is a fantastic way to help you and your family meet your daily protein requirements. †

4 **Superior Protein** – For many people, protein powders can be difficult to digest. For those with dairy or egg sensitivities, whey, casein and egg white protein can cause digestive and other issues, as can brown rice and pea protein for those who don't digest grains or legumes well. †

5 **Diet and Gut-Friendly** – If you're following a gut-supportive diet, leaky gut diet, elimination diet, gluten-free diet, low-carbohydrate diet or a real food diet, this is the perfect protein powder for you. Bone Broth Protein is high in proline and glutamine, which are amino acids that support the digestive system. †

EIGHT GREAT WAYS TO USE BONE BROTH PROTEIN

SMOOTHIES

Add one scoop of Bone Broth Protein to your smoothie every morning for an added 20 grams of gut-friendly protein. †

FOOD BARS AND PROTEIN SNACKS

Make your own homemade protein bars that are great snacks for the whole family and a way to stay healthy while traveling. †

CROCKPOT AND SOUP RECIPES

Use Pure or Turmeric Bone Broth Protein as a direct replacement for bone broth and season yourself with sea salt, parsley and garlic.

ANCIENT GRAINS

Use with quinoa, rice and oats to create a super-grain with a balanced amino acid profile of 20 grams of body-building protein per serving. †

† These statements have not been evaluated by the Food and Drug Administration. This product is not intended to diagnose, treat, cure or prevent any disease.

HEALTHY DESSERTS

Want to support your metabolism and add protein to your dessert? Add protein and gut-friendly nutrients to desserts, such as high-protein cookies and protein puddings. †

NATURAL HEALTH SUPPLEMENT

Use Bone Broth Protein as a supplement for healthy joints, skin, hair, gut health and immune support. †

WORKOUT MEALS

Mix Bone Broth Protein directly in water or mix with dairy, almond or cashew milk plus fruit for a pre-workout and post-workout snack to aid recovery, metabolism and muscle support. †

BONE BROTH CLEANSE

Mix Bone Broth Protein in daily smoothies and juices for an effective full-body cleanse (due to its high levels of glycine and potassium) — see the next chapter for a transformational cleansing program. †

CHAPTER 6

BONE BROTH BODY
CHALLENGE

To maximize the benefits of bone broth — gently detoxifying the body while supporting your gut health, lean muscle, metabolism, skin health, immune system support and even your joints — I strongly recommend that you begin consuming bone broth daily in one form, one way or another. †

The easiest, most healthful and fun way to do this? Take my Bone Broth Body Challenge! There's four unique plans for you to choose from, and you'll be amazed how it will help transform not only your gut health, but your entire body. †

† These statements have not been evaluated by the Food and Drug Administration. This product is not intended to diagnose, treat, cure or prevent any disease.

BONE BROTH BODY CHALLENGE
FOUR PLANS. CHOOSE YOURS.

3-DAY BONE BROTH BURST
- Consume 4-6 servings of bone broth* exclusively for three days, either 20 ounces of homemade bone broth sipped slowly or one scoop of Bone Broth Protein (Pure and/or Turmeric variety) mixed in 12 ounces of water
- If you encounter additional thirst, drink only unsweetened herbal infusions, tea or water

3-DAY BONE BROTH CLEANSE
- Consume one serving of bone broth or Bone Broth Protein for breakfast
- Consume a bone broth smoothie for lunch and dinner
- When thirsty, consume only unsweetened herbal infusions, tea or water

7-DAY BONE BROTH CHALLENGE**
- Prepare and consume 3 recipes per day
- Choose from breakfast/smoothies, snacks or main dishes
- When thirsty, consume only unsweetened herbal infusions, tea or water

30-DAY BONE BROTH TRANSFORMATION**
- 8 a.m. breakfast: consume a Bone Broth Protein smoothie, one serving of bone broth or Bone Broth Protein mixed in water
- 12 p.m. lunch: bone broth main dish or bone broth snack bar
- 6 p.m. dinner: bone broth main dish
- Dessert: limit yourself to 2 bone broth desserts each week

All readers, especially those taking prescription or over-the-counter medications, should consult their physicians before beginning any nutrition or supplement program.

*Remember, 1.5 cups of homemade bone broth is the nutritional equivalent of one scoop of Bone Broth Protein mixed in 12 ounces of water.

**If hungry, consume more bone broth or Bone Broth Protein servings throughout the day.

3-DAY BONE BROTH CLEANSE

DAY 1

Breakfast
8 ounces bone broth or one serving of pure Bone Broth Protein mixed in water or almond milk

Lunch
Bone Broth Blueberry Protein Shake (see recipe on page 59)

Dinner
Mocha Fudge Smoothie (see recipe on page 65)

DAY 2

Breakfast
8 ounces bone broth or one serving of pure Bone Broth Protein mixed in water or almond milk

Lunch
Green Detox Smoothie (see recipe on page 65)

Dinner
Pumpkin Pie Smoothie (see recipe on page 60)

DAY 3

Breakfast
8 ounces bone broth or one serving of pure Bone Broth Protein mixed in water or almond milk

Lunch
Strawberry Coconut Smoothie (see recipe on page 72)

Dinner
Carrot Ginger Smoothie (see recipe on page 62)

7-DAY BONE BROTH CHALLENGE

	MONDAY	TUESDAY	WEDNESDAY
BREAKFAST	Strawberry Coconut Smoothie	8 ounces bone broth*	8 ounces bone broth* mixed with almond milk
LUNCH	Butternut Bisque	Tuna Salad	Bison Cabbage Broth
DINNER	Egg Drop Soup	Avgolemono	Broccoli Cauliflower Soup

3 MEALS PER DAY

8 A.M. BREAKFAST	**12 P.M. LUNCH**	**6 P.M. DINNER**
bone broth smoothie or one serving of pure Bone Broth Protein	bone broth snack/ bar or bone broth main dish	bone broth main dish

THURSDAY	FRIDAY	SATURDAY	SUNDAY
Bone Broth Blueberry Protein Shake	8 ounces bone broth*	Mocha Fudge Smoothie	Gut-Repair Shake
Quinoa-Stuffed Peppers	Indian Curry	Carrot Cake Bar	Chicken Salad
Gingered Beef & Broccoli	Turkey and Rice Congee	Slow Cooker Scalloped Sweet Potatoes	"Noodle" Bowls

*Or one serving of pure Bone Broth Protein mixed in 12 oz. water

30-DAY BONE BROTH TRANSFORMATION†

For best results, repeat this 14-day program another two weeks for a total of four weeks and an additional two days, for a total of 30 days

	DAY 1	DAY 2	DAY 3
8 AM	Bone Broth Blueberry Protein Shake	Pre-Workout Electrolyte Drink	Veggie Frittata
NOON	Chicken Salad	Protein Almond Butter Bar	Bison Cabbage Broth
3 PM	8 ounces bone broth*	8 ounces bone broth*	Golden Tea
6 PM	Butternut Bisque	Avgolemono	Quinoa-Stuffed Peppers + Chocolate Chip Cookies

† These statements have not been evaluated by the Food and Drug Administration. This product is not intended to diagnose, treat, cure or prevent any disease.

8 A.M. BREAKFAST	12 P.M. LUNCH	3 P.M.	6 P.M. DINNER
bone broth smoothie or breakfast recipe	bone broth main dish or bone broth snack bar	8 ounces bone broth or one serving of pure Bone Broth Protein mixed in water	bone broth main dish **Dessert:** limit yourself to 2 bone broth desserts each week

DAY 4	DAY 5	DAY 6	DAY 7
Carrot Ginger Smoothie	Coconut Porridge	Protein Pancakes	Banana Nut Bread
Butternut Bisque	Egg Salad	Post-Workout Muscle-Building Shake	Blueberry Macadamia Bar
8 ounces bone broth*	8 ounces bone broth*	Golden Tea	8 ounces bone broth*
Indian Curry Soup	Meatball Soup	Turkey and Rice Congee + Raspberry Ice Cream	Creamy Tomato Soup

*Or one serving of pure Bone Broth Protein mixed in 12 oz. water

	DAY 8	DAY 9	DAY 10
8 AM	Green Detox Smoothie	High-Protein Oatmeal Raisin	Gut-Repair Shake
NOON	Creamy Tomato Soup	Gingered Beef & Broccoli Soup	Tuna Salad
3 PM	8 ounces bone broth*	Golden Tea	8 ounces bone broth*
6 PM	Slow Cooker Scalloped Sweet Potatoes	"Noodle" Bowls	Meatball Soup + Coconut Macaroons

For best results, repeat this 14-day program another two weeks for a total of four weeks and an additional two days, for a total of 30 days

DAY 11	DAY 12	DAY 13	DAY 14
Egg Tortillas/ Wraps	Oatmeal Cookie Smoothie	Strawberry Coconut Smoothie	Chai Waffles
Almond Fig Bar	Broccoli Cauliflower Soup	Tasty Turkey Burger	Mushroom Miso Soup
8 ounces bone broth*	Golden Tea	8 ounces bone broth*	8 ounces bone broth*
Egg Drop Soup	Quinoa-Stuffed Peppers	Gingered Beef & Broccoli Soup + Frozen Chocolate Bananas	Beef and Butternut Squash Soup

Or one serving of pure Bone Broth Protein mixed in 12 oz. water

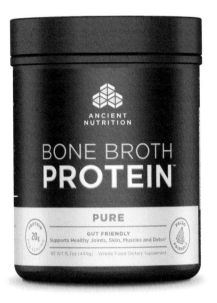

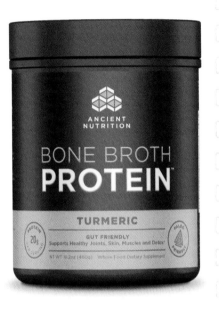

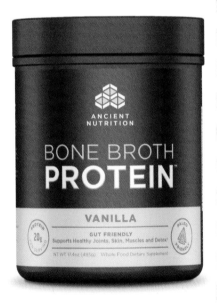

† These statements have not been evaluated by the Food and Drug Administration. This product is not intended to diagnose, treat, cure or prevent any disease.

BONE BROTH PROTEIN™ POWDER

#1 GUT-FRIENDLY PROTEIN POWDER †

BONE BROTH PROTEIN™
PURE AND TURMERIC

- 20g Protein | No Carbs | No Sugars
- Gut-Friendly | Paleo-Friendly | 100% Natural
- Dairy-Free | Soy-Free | Grain-Free | Nut-Free | Gluten-Free
- Amino Acids, Collagen Type II, Glucosamine, Chondroitin, Hyaluronic Acid and Minerals
- Mix in Protein Shakes, Smoothies and Raw Juices. Use It in Your Favorite Recipe or Side, Such as Hummus, Quinoa or Food Bars

- Support Healthy Joints, Skin, Muscles and Detox †

ALSO AVAILABLE NATURALLY DELICIOUS
CHOCOLATE AND VANILLA

- 20g Protein | Low Carbs (2g) | Low Sugars (1g)
- Mixes Easily in Water, Juice, Unsweetened or Sweetened Almond Milk, Coconut Milk, or as Part of a Nutritious Protein Shake
- Add Flavored Bone Broth Protein to Create Protein-Packed Desserts, Pancakes and Snacks!

CHAPTER 7

BONE BROTH RECIPES

BREAKFASTS
AND
SMOOTHIES

PRE-WORKOUT
ELECTROLYTE DRINK

BONE BROTH BLUEBERRY PROTEIN SHAKE

12 ounces coconut
  or almond milk
1 cup frozen blueberries
$\frac{1}{2}$ banana
$\frac{1}{4}$ teaspoon cinnamon,
  optional
1 scoop of pure bone
  broth protein

Place all ingredients in blender and purée until smooth, adding additional nut milk and ice to blend as necessary.

PRE-WORKOUT ELECTROLYTE DRINK

12 ounces coconut water
1 cup frozen mango
$\frac{1}{2}$ cup pineapple
juice of $\frac{1}{2}$ a lime and $\frac{1}{2}$
  a lemon
$\frac{1}{4}$–$\frac{1}{2}$ inch fresh piece of
  ginger
1 scoop of pure bone
  broth protein

Place all ingredients in blender and purée until smooth, adding more coconut water to blend as necessary.

OATMEAL COOKIE SMOOTHIE

½ cup cooked oats
10 raw cashews
12 ounces water
2 dates
pinch cinnamon
pinch sea salt
1 scoop of pure bone
  broth protein

Place all ingredients in a blender and purée until smooth.

PUMPKIN PIE SMOOTHIE

½ cup pumpkin purée
½ cup cooked butternut
  squash
½ teaspoon pumpkin pie
  spice
½ teaspoon vanilla extract
12 ounces coconut milk or
  water
1 scoop of pure bone
  broth protein

Place all ingredients in a blender and purée until smooth, adding extra liquid if needed.

PUMPKIN PIE
SMOOTHIE

CARROT GINGER SMOOTHIE

1 cup steamed carrots
½ cup steamed fennel
½ inch sliced ginger root
12 ounces water
1 scoop of pure bone
  broth protein

Place all ingredients
in a blender and purée
until smooth.

BONE BROTH CLEANSER DRINK

4 carrots (steamed)
4 celery stalks (steamed)
12 ounces of water
handful of cilantro
1 teaspoon turmeric
1 scoop of pure bone
  broth protein powder

After steaming veggies, add all ingredients to blender with water.

PEACH PROBIOTIC SMOOTHIE

½ banana
¾ cup frozen peaches
½ cup goat milk kefir or
  yogurt
1 cup almond or coconut
  milk
½ teaspoon pumpkin pie
  spice or cinnamon
one scoop of pure bone
  broth protein powder
vanilla extract and stevia
  to taste

Place all ingredients in a blender and purée until smooth, adding extra liquid if needed.

PEACH PROBIOTIC
SMOOTHIE

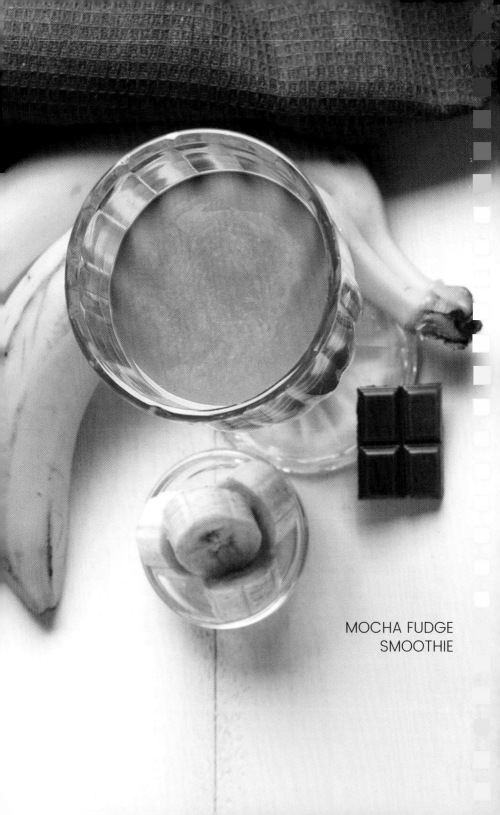

MOCHA FUDGE
SMOOTHIE

MOCHA FUDGE SMOOTHIE

1 cup frozen banana
¼ cup raw cashews
2 tablespoons cocoa powder
1 teaspoon carob powder
1 teaspoon instant coffee
  or espresso powder
12 ounces coconut milk
1 teaspoon raw honey
1 scoop of pure bone
  broth protein
a hint of carob adds extra
  fudginess to this shake

Place all ingredients in blender and purée until smooth, adding water and ice to blend as necessary.

GREEN DETOX SMOOTHIE †

1 cup peeled cucumber
12 ounces coconut water
1 teaspoon minced ginger
½ pear
handful of spinach
1 scoop of pure bone
  broth protein

Place all ingredients in blender and purée until smooth, adding water and ice to blend as necessary.

PROTEIN PANCAKES

SERVES: 4–6   TIME: 20 MINUTES

1 cup applesauce
3 eggs
¼ cup melted coconut oil
⅓ cup coconut flour
4 scoops of pure bone
  broth protein
⅛ teaspoon sea salt

In a medium bowl, whisk applesauce, eggs and oil together thoroughly. Stir in coconut flour, protein powder and sea salt and allow to sit for 5 minutes.

Heat coconut oil in a large skillet over medium heat. Once hot, drop batter into skillet and fry until bubbles form on one side. Flip, finish cooking and enjoy breakfast. These are particularly nice topped with raw honey and cinnamon.

THIN MINT
SMOOTHIE

THIN MINT SMOOTHIE

12 ounces coconut milk
1 tablespoon coconut oil
¼ teaspoon vanilla extract
1 teaspoon raw honey
½ teaspoon peppermint
  extract
2 tablespoons cocoa powder
1 scoop of pure bone
  broth protein

Place all ingredients in blender and purée until smooth, adding water and ice to blend as necessary.

GUT-REPAIR SHAKE †

1 baked pear
12 ounces coconut milk
1 teaspoon minced ginger
1 teaspoon raw honey
1 scoop of pure bone
  broth protein

Preheat oven to 350 F.

Slice pear in half and place face down on baking sheet. Cook for 20 minutes.

Place all ingredients in blender and purée until smooth, adding water and ice to blend as necessary.

† These statements have not been evaluated by the Food and Drug Administration. This product is not intended to diagnose, treat, cure or prevent any disease.

STRAWBERRY COCONUT SMOOTHIE

1 cup frozen strawberries
handful of raw spinach
12 ounces coconut milk
1 tablespoon raw honey
1 teaspoon bee pollen
1 scoop of pure bone
  broth protein

Place all ingredients in blender and purée until smooth, adding water and ice to blend as necessary.

POST-WORKOUT MUSCLE BUILDING SHAKE †

3 raw eggs (optional)
3 tablespoons almond butter
12 ounces plain kefir
1/2 cup gluten-free oats
1 banana
1 scoop of pure bone
  broth protein

Place all ingredients in blender and purée until smooth, adding water and ice to blend as necessary.

† These statements have not been evaluated by the Food and Drug Administration. This product is not intended to diagnose, treat, cure or prevent any disease.

STRAWBERRY
COCONUT
SMOOTHIE

HIGH-PROTEIN OATMEAL RAISIN

SERVES: 1–2   TIME: 20 MINUTES

1 cup gluten-free oats
12 ounces water
1 scoop of pure bone
  broth protein
1/2 cup pitted dates
3/4 cup raw honey
2 tablespoons coconut
  oil, melted
1 teaspoon vanilla extract
2 teaspoons cinnamon
1/2 cup almond butter
3/4 cup raisins

Soak oats overnight in water.

Drain oats and add to a pot along with 12 ounces of water and 1 scoop of pure bone broth protein powder. Heat over medium-high heat.

Bring mixture to a boil and then reduce heat and allow to simmer for 5 minutes.

Place dates, honey, coconut oil, vanilla and cinnamon in food processor and pulse until combined.

Add almond butter and process until combined.

Add mixture from the food processor into the pot and stir before serving.

COCONUT PORRIDGE

SERVES: 1–2   TIME: 15 MINUTES

1 cup almond milk
1 scoop of pure bone
 broth protein
½ cup shredded coconut
1 tablespoon hemp seeds
1 tablespoon chia seeds
1 teaspoon vanilla
¼ teaspoon stevia
½ teaspoon sea salt
top with berries

Place all ingredients in a pot and bring to a boil. Reduce heat and allow to simmer for 5 minutes.

Serve with berries on top.

VEGGIE OMELET

SERVES: 1   TIME: 10 MINUTES

1 garlic clove
½ cup chopped red
  pepper
½ cup chopped green
  pepper
½ cup chopped
  mushroom
¼ cup chopped red
  onion
2 tablespoons butter
1 scoop bone broth
  protein
3 eggs
2 ounces raw cheese
add oregano, chives,
  black pepper, sea
  salt to taste

Sauté garlic, onion, peppers, mushrooms and butter in a saucepan over medium-low heat.

After 5 minutes, mix one scoop of pure bone broth protein with eggs. Add egg mixture.

Shred the cheese on top and let cook for about a minute, then fold into an omelet.

Serve with chives, oregano, black pepper and sea salt to taste.

GOLDEN TEA

SERVES: 2   TIME: 5 MINUTES

8 ounces coconut milk
1 scoop bone broth
  protein
1 tablespoon raw honey
1 teaspoon turmeric
pinch of pumpkin spice
  (or cinnamon and ginger)

Pour coconut milk and
water into the saucepan
and warm for 2 minutes.

Add in raw honey,
turmeric and bone broth
protein for another 2
minutes.

Stir and pour into
glasses.

CHAI WAFFLES

SERVES: 4-6   TIME: 20 MINUTES

3 eggs
¼ cup coconut oil
¾ cup applesauce
1 tablespoon vanilla
  extract
⅓ cup coconut flour
4 scoops of pure bone
  broth protein
⅛ teaspoon sea salt
½ teaspoon each:
  cardamom, ginger,
  cinnamon
¼ teaspoon each:
  nutmeg, cloves

Whisk eggs, oil, applesauce and vanilla together. Stir in remaining ingredients and allow to sit for 5 minutes.

Cook according to waffle iron instructions.

EGG TORTILLAS/WRAPS

SERVES: 4–6 TIME: 25 MINUTES

2 eggs
¹/₂ cup coconut milk
¹/₄ cup coconut oil
1 cup arrowroot starch
¹/₃ cup coconut flour
4 scoops of pure bone
  broth protein
¹/₈ teaspoon sea salt

In a medium bowl, whisk eggs thoroughly and add milk and oil.

Add arrowroot, flour, protein powder and sea salt and combine thoroughly. Let mixture sit for 5 minutes.

Heat coconut oil in a large skillet over medium heat. Add batter by ¹/₃ cup to pan and cook 2–4 minutes each side. Cool to room temperature and refrigerate.

VEGGIE FRITTATA

SERVES: 4   TIME: 40 MINUTES

1 scoop of pure bone
  broth protein mixed in
  8 ounces water
$\frac{1}{2}$ teaspoon sea salt
$\frac{1}{2}$ red onion, diced
1 cup small broccoli
  florets
1 cup sliced mushrooms
$\frac{1}{2}$ red pepper, diced
8 eggs
1 tablespoon minced
  fresh basil
$\frac{1}{4}$ teaspoon crushed red
  pepper or chipotle
  flakes, optional

In a large, all-metal sauté pan over medium-high heat, heat bone broth and sea salt to a simmer. Add veggies and simmer for 8 minutes, uncovered. Reduce heat to low. Turn oven to low broil.

In a medium bowl, whisk eggs, basil and optional pepper flakes together thoroughly. Add egg mixture to pan and stir to combine.

Cover and cook on stovetop for 10-15 minutes. Broil for 3-7 minutes, watching carefully, until eggs are set.

BANANA NUT BREAD

SERVES: 6–8   TIME: 55 MINUTES

4 eggs
3 medium overly ripe
  bananas, mashed
¼ cup honey
¼ cup coconut milk
1 tablespoon vanilla extract
2 teaspoons baking soda
2¼ cups almond flour
½ teaspoon sea salt
½ teaspoon cinnamon
1 scoop of pure bone
  broth protein

Preheat oven to 350 F.
In a bowl, mix eggs,
banana, honey, coconut
milk and vanilla.

In a separate bowl,
combine the remaining
ingredients.

Combine both mixtures
and stir until well
incorporated.

Grease a bread pan and
pour in batter. Bake for
35–50 minutes.

MAIN DISHES

BUTTERNUT BISQUE

SERVES: 4   TIME: 1 HOUR

2 tablespoons coconut oil
1 red onion, chopped
1 large butternut squash,
  peeled and chopped
2 red peppers, chopped
2 cloves garlic, smashed
$\frac{1}{2}$ cup sherry
4 cups chicken bone broth
  or 3 scoops of pure bone
  broth protein mixed in
  36 ounces water
$\frac{1}{2}$ teaspoon sea salt
1 sprig thyme
1 cup chopped celery
4 scoops of bone broth
  protein
1 can coconut milk
$\frac{1}{2}$ teaspoon each paprika
  and cayenne

In a medium pot, heat coconut oil over medium heat. Once melted, add onion, butternut, red pepper and garlic and sauté for 10–15 minutes, until browned and fragrant.

Deglaze pan with sherry and broth. Add sea salt, thyme and celery, and simmer for 20 minutes.

Remove sprig of thyme and purée with bone broth in an immersion blender.

Add coconut milk, paprika and cayenne, and heat on low, stirring to combine.

QUINOA-STUFFED PEPPERS

SERVES: 2–4   TIME: 45 MINUTES

2 cups water
1 scoop of bone broth
  protein
1 cup quinoa, rinsed
  and drained
2 bell peppers, halved
  and seeded
1 teaspoon olive oil plus
  additional for drizzling
1 onion, chopped
1 zucchini, chopped
2 tablespoons minced
  garlic
1 tablespoon dried Italian
  seasoning
1/2 cup fresh parsley,
  chopped

Preheat oven to 450 degrees F.

Combine water, broth and quinoa in a medium saucepan. Bring to a boil. Reduce heat to low, cover and cook for 15 minutes. Remove from heat and let stand, covered, for 5 minutes. Fluff with fork and set aside.

Meanwhile, sprinkle bell peppers with sea salt and pepper. Place on baking sheet and roast cut side down until skin begins to char, about 20 minutes. Remove from oven and reduce oven temperature to 375 degrees F.

While bell peppers roast, heat oil in a skillet over medium heat. Add onion, zucchini, garlic and Italian seasoning. Season with salt and pepper. Cook, stirring occasionally, until vegetables are tender, 10-12 minutes. Add reserved quinoa. Sprinkle with parsley and stir to combine.

Turn bell peppers cut side up and fill halves evenly with quinoa mixture. Drizzle with oil as desired. Heat in the oven until warmed through.

TURKEY AND RICE CONGEE

SERVES: 4-6   TIME: 1.5 HOURS

4 cups chicken or turkey
  bone broth or 3 scoops of
  pure bone broth protein
  mixed in 36 ounces water
4 cups water
1 cup brown rice
1 tablespoon grated
  fresh ginger
1 tablespoon grated
  fresh turmeric
1 teaspoon sea salt
3 carrots, peeled and
  chopped into circles
1 large red onion, diced
1 bunch kale, washed, torn
  into pieces, stems
  discarded or saved for
  juicing
2 garlic cloves, pressed or
  minced
2 cups shredded turkey

In a large pot over medium heat, bring broth, water and rice to a simmer. Add ginger and turmeric. Reduce heat to medium low and cook, partly covered, for 45 minutes.

Add sea salt, carrots, onion, kale, garlic and turkey to soup and simmer, partly covered, for 25 minutes.

Remove from heat, stir in protein powder and serve.

BISON CABBAGE BROTH

SERVES: 8–10   TIME: 45 MINUTES

ground bison
  (1.5 pounds)
2 onions, diced
32 ounces beef broth or
  3 scoops of bone broth
  protein mixed in 32
  ounces water
2 bay leaves
1 cabbage, chopped
  thinly
12 carrots, sliced in
  rounds
5 potatoes, diced
sea salt and pepper

Heat a large pot on medium high and add ground bison. Stir until partly cooked through. Add onions and finish cooking bison.

Add remaining ingredients and cover. Stir occasionally, reducing to medium heat once it simmers. Cook for 30 minutes and serve.

MEATBALL SOUP

SERVES: 4–6   TIME: 50 MINUTES

1½ pound ground bison
  or beef
2 eggs, whisked
½ teaspoon sea salt
1 teaspoon paprika or
  cayenne
2 tablespoons coconut oil
4 cups bone broth or 3
  scoops pure bone broth
  protein mixed
  in 36 ounces water
2 cups water
1 teaspoon sea salt
2 bay leaves
4 carrots, washed and
  chopped
1 large sweet potato,
  chopped
1 cup green beans
1 cup green peas
2 tomatoes, chopped
sea salt and pepper to
  taste
chopped green onions
  to top

Mix meat, eggs, ½ teaspoon sea salt, and paprika or cayenne together. Roll into small meatballs.

In a large pot, heat oil over medium heat. Add meatballs and cook for 5–8 minutes, just until they brown.

Add broth, water, sea salt, bay leaves, carrots and sweet potatoes. Bring to a simmer over medium-high heat.

Add remaining ingredients and simmer for 20 minutes or until sweet potatoes are done.

INDIAN CURRY SOUP

SERVES: 4　TIME: 35 MINUTES

6 cups chicken bone broth or 3 scoops of pure bone broth protein mixed in 36 ounces water

1 tablespoon each: grated fresh turmeric and ginger

2–3 tablespoons Indian curry powder

1 yellow onion, chopped

2 cups small cauliflower florets

2 red peppers, chopped

1 teaspoon cayenne pepper, optional

1 can coconut milk

In a large pot over medium heat, bring bone broth, turmeric and ginger to a simmer.

Add curry, onions, cauliflower, peppers and cayenne. Bring to a simmer, decrease heat to medium low and simmer 15 minutes. Add coconut milk, stir to combine and cook 5–10 more minutes.

EGG DROP SOUP

SERVES: 4   TIME: 20 MINUTES

4 cups bone broth or 3 scoops pure bone broth protein mixed in 36 ounces water

4 cups water

2 baby bok choy, thinly sliced

½ cup sliced mushrooms, sliced

1 tablespoon ground ginger

1 tablespoon Bragg's liquid aminos

1 teaspoon sea salt

1 teaspoon ground white pepper

4 large eggs

2 egg yolks

green onions, thinly sliced

In a medium pot, bring broth and water to a very low simmer. Add in bok choy, mushrooms, ginger, liquid aminos, salt and pepper and simmer for 10–12 minutes.

Whisk eggs and egg yolks in a small bowl and, holding a fork over the bowl, gently pour eggs through the tines of the fork.

Lightly whisk broth and gently stir in green onions.

Ladle into bowls and top with more green onions if desired.

AVGOLEMONO

SERVES: 4   TIME: 30 MINUTES

4 cups bone broth or 3
  scoops of pure bone broth
  protein mixed in
  36 ounces water
2 cups water
1 cup brown rice
1 teaspoon sea salt
3 eggs
juice of 2 large lemons
2 cups shredded cooked
  chicken

In a large pot over medium heat, add broth, water, rice and sea salt. Cook for 30 minutes or until rice is tender. Reduce heat to medium low.

In a medium bowl, whisk eggs and lemon juice together until lighter in color.

Take 2 cups of liquid from soup, and, stirring constantly, carefully add it in a thin stream to eggs and juice.

While stirring soup, add egg mixture to simmering pot and stir until thickened, about 2-3 minutes.

Remove from heat and serve.

CREAMY TOMATO SOUP

SERVES: 6-8   TIME: 20 MINUTES

3 cloves garlic, pressed
  or minced
1 tablespoon coconut oil
two 28-ounce BPA-free
  cans salt-free diced
  tomatoes
one 14-ounce can
  coconut milk
½ teaspoon sea salt
2 teaspoons apple cider
  vinegar
4 scoops pure bone
  broth protein
fresh basil, minced
fresh cracked pepper

In a medium pot over medium-low heat, sauté garlic in oil for 5 minutes or until lightly browned.

Add tomatoes, coconut milk, sea salt and vinegar, stirring to combine.

Cook until hot. Top each serving with fresh basil and fresh cracked pepper.

BEEF AND BUTTERNUT SQUASH SOUP

SERVES: 6   TIME: 35 MINUTES

6 cups beef bone broth or 4 scoops of pure bone broth protein mixed in 48 ounces water

2 cups water

1½ teaspoons powdered ginger

1 teaspoon chipotle pepper

1 teaspoon cumin

½ teaspoon sea salt

1 pound beef, sliced or cubed

1 yellow onion

1 medium butternut squash

In a large pot over medium heat, bring broth with spices and sea salt to a simmer.

Add remaining ingredients and return to a simmer. Reduce heat to low and simmer for 25 minutes.

GINGERED BEEF & BROCCOLI SOUP

SERVES: 4   TIME: 25 MINUTES

2 cups beef bone broth or one scoop of pure bone broth protein
1½ pounds ribeye or top sirloin, sliced
1 head broccoli, chopped
1 large red onion, chopped
1 tablespoon grated fresh ginger
2 cloves garlic, pressed or minced
½ teaspoon sea salt
coconut aminos

In a large saucepan over medium-high heat, bring bone broth to a rolling simmer.

Add beef, broccoli, onion, ginger, garlic and sea salt. Cover and cook for 8-10 minutes, until broccoli is just tender.

Remove lid and stir until beef is done and broccoli is tender, another 5-8 minutes.

Serve with coconut aminos.

TASTY TURKEY BURGERS

SERVES: 2–4   TIME: 20 MINUTES

½ diced onion
1 pound ground turkey
1 scoop bone broth
  protein
1 teaspoon sea salt
½ teaspoon garlic powder
½ teaspoon turmeric
  powder
¼ teaspoon paprika
¼ teaspoon coriander
¼ teaspoon black pepper
romaine lettuce or
  sprouted grain bun

Sauté onion over medium heat until tender (8–10 minutes).

Combine onion with turkey, bone broth protein and seasonings.

Form into four patties and grill until done.

Serve on romaine lettuce wrap or sprouted grain bun.

MUSHROOM MISO SOUP

SERVES: 2–4   TIME: 35 MINUTES

4 cups chicken bone
  broth or 3 scoops
  of pure bone broth
  protein mixed
  in 36 ounces water
1 cup baby portabella
  mushrooms
1/2 red onion, chopped
3 cloves garlic, pressed
  or minced
1 tablespoon grated
  ginger
1/4 cup dried wakame
3 tablespoons mellow
  white or garbanzo miso
half-bunch scallions,
  chopped

In a medium pot over medium-high heat, bring broth to a rolling simmer. Add mushrooms, onion, garlic, ginger and wakame. Reduce heat to medium and simmer for 15 minutes. Reduce heat to medium-low and remove 1½ cups of broth.

Whisk broth into miso and add to soup. Hold at low heat for 5 minutes before serving.

Top each bowl with scallions.

BROCCOLI CAULIFLOWER SOUP

SERVES: 4   TIME: 30 MINUTES

8 cups chicken bone broth or 5 scoops of pure bone broth protein mixed in 60 ounces water

1 tablespoon grated turmeric

2 cloves garlic, pressed or minced

½ teaspoon sea salt

1 head of broccoli, chopped into small pieces

1 head of cauliflower, chopped into small pieces

1 medium yellow onion, diced

1 cup dry, raw cashews, ground into powder

pepper to taste

In a large pot, heat broth, turmeric, garlic and sea salt to a simmer over medium heat.

When simmering, add broccoli, cauliflower and onion. Simmer for 10 minutes.

Add ground cashews and pepper and stir for 5 minutes. Remove from heat and stir in protein powder.

SLOW COOKER SCALLOPED SWEET POTATOES

SERVES: 6–8   PREP: 15 MINUTES   TIME: 3 HOURS

butter
smashed garlic clove
3 large sweet potatoes,
  sliced thin
1 yellow onion, diced
$1/2$ teaspoon sea salt
$1^1/2$ tablespoons chili
  powder
1 teaspoon cumin
2 cups shredded goat or
  sheep milk cheese
$1^1/2$ cups coconut milk
2 eggs
1 scoop of pure bone
  broth protein

Butter the inside of the crock pot and rub with smashed garlic clove. Mince garlic clove and set aside.

Start with one layer of sweet potato slices. Top with some onions, garlic, sea salt, chili powder, cumin and cheese. Keep layering sweet potatoes, onions, garlic, spices and cheese.

Whisk egg, bone broth and protein powder together, and pour over sweet potato mixture.

Cover, turn crockpot to high and cook for $2^1/2$–3 hours.

"NOODLE" BOWLS

SERVES: 4   TIME: 40 MINUTES

1 spaghetti squash
1 tablespoon coconut oil
4 ounces beef or chicken, chopped
1 large onion, sliced
2 carrots, peeled, halved and chopped into sticks
1 head of broccoli, cut into small florets
2 cloves garlic, pressed or minced
1 zucchini, sliced
1½ cups sliced mushrooms
3 eggs
1 scoop of pure bone broth protein
1 tablespoon coconut aminos

Preheat oven to 425 F.

Split spaghetti squash in half carefully. Place squash cut side down on a pan. Cover with foil and bake for 20–30 minutes or until tender.

Heat a large pot over medium heat. Add coconut oil, meat, onion and carrots, and stir, cooking for 5 minutes.

Add broccoli and garlic and cook 5 more minutes.

Add zucchini and mushrooms and cook 5 more minutes.

Break eggs into a bowl, mix in pure bone broth protein powder and add to pot, stirring constantly to cook eggs and distribute evenly.

Turn off heat once eggs are cooked, add liquid aminos and stir.

Remove squash from oven and carefully scoop "noodles" into 4 bowls. Top with veggie-egg mixture and enjoy!

CHICKEN SALAD

SERVES: 1-2   TIME: 10 MINUTES

cooked whole chicken
  breast, shredded or cut
  into small pieces
1 celery stalk, chopped
6-8 grapes, sliced
small handful walnuts,
  chopped
1 tablespoon kefir
1 teaspoon dijon mustard
1 scoop of pure bone
  broth protein
1 teaspoon black pepper
$\frac{1}{2}$ teaspoon sea salt
fresh spinach or lettuce

Mix chicken, chopped
celery, grapes and a
small handful of walnuts
in a bowl.

Mix in kefir, mustard,
bone broth protein,
pepper and salt.

Serve on bed of spinach
or romaine lettuce.

EGG SALAD

SERVES: 2–4   TIME: 10 MINUTES

5 hard-boiled eggs
¼ cup celery
¼ cup sprouted pecans
½ cup Vegenaise
¼ cup raisins
1 scoop of pure bone
  broth protein
sea salt and black pepper

Chop eggs, celery and pecans.

Combine all ingredients together.

Serve chilled.

TUNA SALAD

SERVES: 2   PREP: 10 MINUTES   TIME: 1 HOUR

1 can (5-6 ounces) wild-
  caught tuna, drained
  and flaked
¼ cup organic mayonnaise
½ scoop of pure bone broth
  protein
1 rib celery, finely chopped
2 tablespoons minced onion
1 tablespoon Dijon mustard
1-2 tablespoons unsweetened
  dried cranberries
fresh lemon juice
sea salt and pepper

In a bowl, combine tuna, mayo, bone broth protein, celery, onion, mustard and cranberries.

Season with lemon juice, salt and pepper to taste. Mix until well combined.

Chill for at least 1 hour before serving.

TUNA SALAD

SNACKS
AND BARS

SWEET POTATO HUMMUS

SERVES: 4   PREP: 45 MINUTES   TIME: 2 HOURS

1½ pounds sweet potato
½ cup tahini
1 scoop of pure bone
  broth protein
2 large garlic cloves
¼ cup lime
2 tablespoons lemon juice
1 teaspoon sea salt
½ teaspoon pepper
¼ cup cilantro (garnish)
olive oil (garnish)

Chop the sweet potatoes into large chunks and add to a pot of boiling water.

Let mixture boil for 30–40 minutes or until sweet potatoes are soft.

Drain the water and sweet potatoes through a sieve and carefully peel the skins off of the sweet potatoes.

Add the sweet potatoes to the food processor with tahini, bone broth powder, garlic, lime, lemon, salt and pepper and purée until smooth.

Refrigerate the hummus in an airtight container until cooled and then garnish with olive oil and chopped cilantro before serving.

ALMOND CACAO BAR

SERVES: 6-8   PREP: 15 MINUTES   TIME: 2 HOURS

1 cup almond butter
$\frac{1}{2}$ cup raw honey
1 teaspoon vanilla
$\frac{1}{8}$ teaspoon sea salt
1 cup oats
4 scoops bone broth
  protein
$\frac{1}{2}$ cup cacao nibs

Whisk together almond butter, honey, vanilla and sea salt.

Add oats, protein powder and cacao nibs and combine. Form into bar or cookie shapes and refrigerate.

BLUEBERRY MACADAMIA BAR

SERVES: 6   PREP: 15 MINUTES   TIME: 2 HOURS

$\frac{1}{2}$ cup melted coconut
  butter
$\frac{1}{4}$ cup raw honey
1 teaspoon vanilla extract
$\frac{1}{8}$ teaspoon sea salt
4 scoops of pure bone
  broth protein
$\frac{1}{2}$ cup dried blueberries
$\frac{1}{2}$ cup macadamias,
  chopped
3 tablespoons water

Whisk together butter, honey, vanilla and sea salt. Add protein powder and combine. Add remaining ingredients and combine.

Pour into a greased loaf pan. Refrigerate for 1-2 hours and then cut into bar or cookie shapes.

ALMOND FIG BAR

SERVES: 4   PREP: 15 MINUTES   TIME: 4 HOURS

1 cup dried figs
1 cup almond butter
1 tablespoon flax meal
2 scoops pure bone broth
  protein
2 tablespoons raw honey

Line an 8 x 8 baking pan with parchment paper and set aside.

Add all ingredients to food processor and blend until dough starts to form in to a ball.

Press the dough evenly into the pan and refrigerate for 3-4 hours or until the bars set.

Cut into squares and store in an airtight container.

GLUTEN-FREE BLUEBERRY MUFFINS

SERVES: 12   PREP: 20 MINUTES   TIME: 45 MINUTES

1¾ cups almond flour
½ teaspoon baking soda
pinch of sea salt
3 eggs
⅓ cup honey
1 teaspoon vanilla extract
2 scoops pure bone broth
  protein
5-6 tablespoons coconut
  oil or ghee, melted
1 cup fresh blueberries

Preheat oven to 350 degrees F.

In a bowl, combine almond flour, baking soda and sea salt.
In a separate bowl, combine combine eggs, honey, vanilla, protein powder and coconut oil/ghee.

Combine both mixtures together. Once well incorporated, add blueberries and mix.

Fill a muffin pan with liners. Fill each liner with batter.

Bake in oven for 20-30 minutes.

CARROT CAKE BAR

SERVES: 10–12   TIME: 35 MINUTES

1 cup pitted and halved
  dates
½ cup melted coconut oil
1 teaspoon vanilla extract
2 teaspoons cinnamon
2 eggs
¼ teaspoon sea salt
3 scoops pure bone broth
  protein
1½ cups shredded carrots
½ cup walnut pieces
1½ cups oats
¾ cup raisins

Preheat oven to 375 degrees F. Line a 9-inch pie pan or 8-inch square dish with parchment paper.

Blend together dates, coconut oil, vanilla and cinnamon.

In a medium mixing bowl, whisk eggs, sea salt and protein powder together until eggs are lighter in color.

Add date mixture and whisk to combine. Add remaining ingredients and stir to combine. Bake for 20 minutes or until done.

PECAN PIE BAR

SERVES: 6   PREP: 15 MINUTES   TIME: 2 HOURS

1¼ cups pecans
3 scoops pure bone broth
  protein powder
¼ teaspoon sea salt
1 cup halved and pitted
  dates
1 tablespoon raw honey
1 tablespoon melted
  coconut oil
1 teaspoon vanilla extract

Place pecans in food
processor and pulse
until in fine pieces.
Add protein powder
and sea salt; pulse until
combined.

Add dates, honey, oil
and vanilla, and process
until combined and
sticky.

Form into bar shapes and
refrigerate until ready to
eat.

APPLE PIE BAR

SERVES: 8–10   PREP: 15 MINUTES   TIME: 2 HOURS

½ cup walnuts
½ cup cashews
4 scoops pure bone broth
  protein powder
2 teaspoons apple pie spice
zest of half a lemon
¼ teaspoon sea salt
1 cup pitted and halved dates
1½ cups loosely packed dried
  apples
1 tablespoon coconut oil
1 teaspoon vanilla extract

Place walnuts and cashews in food processor and pulse until in fine pieces.

Add protein powder, spice, lemon zest and sea salt, and pulse until combined.

Add dates, apples, oil and vanilla, and process until combined and sticky.

Form into bar shapes and refrigerate until ready to eat.

DESSERTS

FROZEN CHOCOLATE BANANAS

SERVES: 4   PREP: 15 MINUTES   TIME: 1 HOUR

2 bananas
4 popsicle sticks or
  chop sticks
$\frac{1}{2}$ cup coconut oil
$\frac{1}{4}$ cup raw honey
$\frac{1}{3}$ cup cocoa powder
1 scoop pure bone
  broth protein powder

Slice bananas in half and insert a popsicle stick. Place on a plate in the freezer.

Melt coconut oil and whisk in honey, then cocoa powder and protein powder. Allow to cool to room temperature.

Remove bananas from freezer and drizzle mixture over frozen bananas thoroughly.

Return to freezer until chocolate is fully frozen and ready to enjoy.

RASPBERRY ICE CREAM

SERVES: 4   PREP: 5 MINUTES   TIME: 1 HOUR

1½ cans full-fat coconut
  milk
½ cup raw honey
1 scoop pure bone
  broth protein
½ teaspoon vanilla
1½ cups raspberries

Place coconut milk, honey, bone broth protein and vanilla in a high-speed blender, and blend on high for 2 minutes.

Add raspberries and blend again, just until mostly smooth. A few raspberry chunks are nice.

Freeze according to ice cream maker manufacturer's instructions.

CHOCOLATE
CHIP COOKIES

CHOCOLATE CHIP COOKIES

SERVES: 6   PREP: 10 MINUTES   TIME: 2 HOURS

1½ cups almond butter
¼ cup raw honey
1 teaspoon vanilla extract
¼ teaspoon sea salt
1 scoop pure bone
  broth protein
½ cup dark chocolate
  chips

Stir almond butter, honey, vanilla and sea salt together. Add protein powder and combine thoroughly.

Stir in chocolate chips and refrigerate. Form into cookie shapes and enjoy.

BANANA CHIA PUDDING

SERVES: 3–4   PREP: 10 MINUTES   TIME: 20 MINUTES

1 cup coconut milk
¼ cup chia seeds ground
5 tablespoons raw honey
1 banana
1 teaspoon vanilla extract
1 scoop pure bone broth
  protein
¼ teaspoon pumpkin
  spice or cinnamon

Add all ingredients to a food processor or blender and blend for 1 minute.

Refrigerate for 10–15 minutes before serving.

CASHEW COOKIE

SERVES:6   PREP: 15 MINUTES   TIME: 1 HOUR

1¼ cups cashews
1 scoop pure bone
  broth protein
¼ teaspoon sea salt
1 cup halved and pitted
  dates
1 tablespoon raw honey
1 tablespoon melted
  coconut oil

Place cashews in food processor and pulse until in fine pieces. Add protein powder and sea salt; pulse until combined.

Add dates, honey and oil, and process until combined and sticky.

Form into bar shapes and refrigerate until ready to eat.

KEY LIME PIE

SERVES: 6–8   PREP: 15 MINUTES   TIME: 2 HOURS

1¼ cup cashews
1 scoop pure bone
  broth protein
zest of 2 limes
¼ teaspoon sea salt
1 cup dates
1 tablespoon raw honey
1 tablespoon melted
  coconut oil
2 tablespoons lime juice

Place cashews in food processor and pulse until in fine pieces. Add protein powder, lime zest and salt, and pulse until combined.

Add dates, honey, oil, juice and vanilla, and process until combined and sticky.

Pour and press into a pie dish and refrigerate until set, at least 2 hours.

COCONUT MACAROONS

6 egg whites
1 scoop of pure bone
  broth protein
¼ teaspoon sea salt
½ cup raw honey
1 tablespoon vanilla
  extract
3 cups coconut flakes

In mixing bowl, whisk egg whites, bone broth protein and sea salt until peaks form in the eggs.

Add in raw honey, vanilla and coconut.

Form batter into circles and drop onto parchment paper on a cookie sheet.

Pinch off each at the top like a chocolate kiss.

Bake at 350 degrees F for 10–15 minutes until lightly browned.

CHOCOLATE MILK SHAKE

SERVES: 1   TIME: 5 MINUTES

1 cup frozen banana
¼ cup raw cashews
2 tablespoons cocoa
  powder
12 ounces coconut,
  almond or cashew milk
1 tablespoon raw honey
1 scoop of pure bone
  broth protein
vanilla extract to taste

Place all ingredients in blender and purée until smooth, adding water and ice to blend as necessary.

INDEX

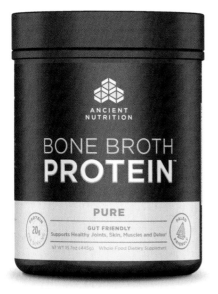

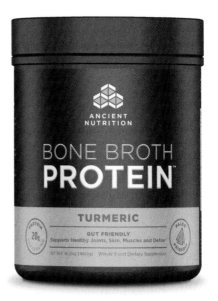

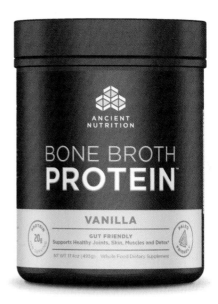

† These statements have not been evaluated by the Food and Drug Administration. This product is not intended to diagnose, treat, cure or prevent any disease.

BONE BROTH PROTEIN™ POWDER

#1 GUT-FRIENDLY PROTEIN POWDER †

BONE BROTH PROTEIN™
PURE AND TURMERIC

- 20g Protein | No Carbs | No Sugars
- Gut-Friendly | Paleo-Friendly | 100% Natural
- Dairy-Free | Soy-Free | Grain-Free | Nut-Free | Gluten-Free
- Amino Acids, Collagen Type II, Glucosamine, Chondroitin, Hyaluronic Acid and Minerals
- Mix in Protein Shakes, Smoothies and Raw Juices. Use It in Your Favorite Recipe or Side, Such as Hummus, Quinoa or Food Bars

- Support Healthy Joints, Skin, Muscles and Detox †

ALSO AVAILABLE NATURALLY DELICIOUS
CHOCOLATE AND VANILLA

- 20g Protein | Low Carbs (2g) | Low Sugars (1g)
- Mixes Easily in Water, Juice, Unsweetened or Sweetened Almond Milk, Coconut Milk, or as Part of a Nutritious Protein Shake
- Add Flavored Bone Broth Protein to Create Protein-Packed Desserts, Pancakes and Snacks!